MW00776035

Jo Taylor

STRANGE FIRE

Reflections on Family and Faith

Best Wishes —
Jo Taylor

for Wally and Cortney

We only live, only suspire
Consumed by either fire or fire.
—T.S. Eliot, "Little Gidding," *Four Quartets*

CONTENTS

WHERE I'M FROM

After George Ella Lyons

I am from tenant farmers,
from mules and corn-filled wagons.
I am from swamp and river—
muddy, rushing, speaking life.
I am from cotton bloom and boll,
representing work and survival,
from burlap sack and scale,
the gin that mined the seeds.
I am from lard and side meat,
from feed-sack dresses and Singer machines.
I am from storytellers and a porch culture,
from "Y'all come" and "What ails you?"
I am from peanut-boilings and cane-grindings,
from hog-killings and sweet tea.
I am from dreams and prophecies and Holy Ghost fire.
I am from foot tub and outhouse,
from Sears and Roebuck catalogues and homemade lye soap.
I'm from turpentine cups and bleeding pine trees,
from Daddy's back plasters and Mama's rough hands.
I'm from fuzzy television and static radio,
from memories, sun-washed and weathered
like a rusty Cadillac de Ville.

THE SEPTAD

With Line from Mary Oliver

I'm child seven, born the seventh month.
I do not have to be good
because I am already perfect, you see.
The prime, boasting the seven wonders of the world
on everyone's bucket list, singing of the seven colors
of the rainbow and of the seven holes in your head.
(Go ahead, right now, and number them.)
I am Joshua's horn blown seven times at Jericho,
I'm trumpet seven at the resurrection of the dead.
I am finished, complete, whole. I am luck and mystique,
the winning jackpot at the gambler's slot.
Popular, powerful, holy, I'm the septad, and
I do not have to be good.

CREDO

I believe in love. In a mother's love.
Especially a mother's love. Like that of Demeter
who searched across time and eternity to succor
her wounded offspring. I believe in God's love.
That nothing can separate us from it. Not the evil one.
Not even death. And I believe we are born to hunger for God.

I believe in music. In its power to quicken like ice, to soothe like
lavender. To affect change as did Lady Day's jazz vocal about
strange fruit swaying from the South's poplar trees;
to transport us to other realms where *trouble melts*
like lemon drops or to where Elvis' ghost strolls Memphis streets
and still pays visits to Graceland.

I believe what goes around comes around, that we reap
what we sow. I believe it with all my being. When we harm
children. Even the unborn. When we hurt the mentally and
physically challenged. The aged.

And speaking of kids, I do not adhere to the argument
violent imagery has little effect on them. I believe it seeps
into their psyches, sticking like aphids, staining
like mulberries. What's more, I believe in Nature, that She is the
great teacher, that kids should spend their time with her.
To give her occasion to instruct, heal, restore.

I believe in hard work, in challenge-based learning. In Wendell
Berry's affirmation that *the impeded stream is the one that sings.* I
believe in failure, but I also believe in second chances.

I believe in laughter. In lightening up. In going on picnics, flying
kites, attending concerts, picking strawberries
with little boys, dancing in the rain on your daddy's toes.

I believe the pen is mightier than the sword. That words
have power. And consequences. That my daddy did not realize
the stinger he embedded when he rejoined that I, his seventh
born, thought myself the Queen of Sheba. Though after a half-
century, I sometimes massage the scar, I have forgiven him.

I believe in forgiveness. Over and again. Seventy times
over. Because bitterness begets bad blood.

I believe that we help the impoverished, that we are not
to harvest the corners of our fields nor to strip the last grape pods
from our vines but are to leave remnants for the poor and the
stranger. I believe it not the state's responsibility to take care of
the needy, that it does because we have forfeited
our privilege, our right, our inheritance.

I believe in the kindness of strangers. In good Samaritans, those
who reach out to families stranded in a desert place
after a long starless night, the morning arriving as heavy
as the darkness.

And I believe in Christ. In the promise of life eternal
through Him, in how He suffered and died at the hands
of sinful man, was buried in a borrowed tomb, and then arose
on the third day that we can wear his imputed righteousness, that
we be justified before a Holy God. Some things
you can't explain. You simply believe.

TAKES ON LITTLE WOMEN

I want to do something splendid before I go into my castle—something heroic, or wonderful—that won't be forgotten after I'm dead…I think I shall write books…
—Jo March in Louisa May Alcott's Little Women

On Goodyear's tire, doused white for make-shift
flower garden, she poses, a raven-haired two-year-old,
holding her rubber doll. At home in the fenced-in
carefully-swept yard, the fresh dirt inviting curiosity
to her pudgy, bare feet. A perfect shot, her frame
just off-center, her black and white flour-sack dress
complementing the split-rails, her grin in focus.

Somewhere across dirt roads beyond picture's
overgrown hedge and towering power lines, her sister,
twenty-two and tall, smiling, keen cat-eyes drawing
in worlds from books and imagination. A reel captures her
milling about her two-room school house, coaxing, praising,
prodding, like a mother bird encouraging her fledglings to fly.

Expose again the little girl in black and white, christened
Jo by her big sister. Destined by name to teach and war
with words. A sister's blessing and curse.
Like a jester bearing missives from the king
or prophet declaring truth and consequence.

A CONSTITUTION

I like tanned, bald heads. A tall, Herculean man. A lean style.
I like pretty clothes and line-dried, lemony-smelling sheets.
I like yellow-meated watermelons that taste of summer.

I hate pecan pie with hulls in it. Playing cards. My oldest sister's
limping from an auto accident years ago. The sight
of the paltry, the diseased, with twisted frames. I hate paying off
charge cards for merchandise long gone.

I like spider lilies in autumn. Also called naked ladies
or resurrection flowers. Naked because they grow long
stems with no leaves. Resurrection because they wake
from a long slumber, bursting with blazing-red curls.

I hate lies as did Marlow, arguing there's a taint of death
in them. I hate racists, bigots, bullies and bugs. Brothers
with all the solutions. Politicians caving to special
interests, self-serving like Chaucer's Chanticleer.

I like Jazz. The Blues. Festivals in springtime. I like art. *Ars longa,*
vita brevis. I like poetry. Robert Penn Warren
and Seamus Heaney. I like family stories, hearing
my four-year-old daughter had missed me, had not eaten
when I was away.

I hate heavy makeup. Dyed, jet-black hair like a sooty heart.
Reptilian toenails. I hate cynicism and pessimism and
down-turning smiles. When people are lonely. When they're in
chaos. When they cry.

I like it when the light goes on for a student reading Faulkner.
When discussion happens in Sunday school. I like weighty ser-
mons that disturb. I like warm weather's showers,
its lightning shows. I like watching flowers grow.
And children. Their parents, too.

I hate total darkness. The darkness of despair. Holes that swallow
you up. I hate snakes, all of them, including the one in Eden's
garden. Especially him. The shrewd one.
The crafty one. The father of lies. I hate lies.

I like the rust-colored, gray-crowned kestrel, airborne, hanging
in the skies, adjusting its controls, dispelling the turbulence.
I like winter. Woolen socks, woolen hats, woolen mittens.
The fire that cracks and spews. You and me snuggling.

This is me. I own it.

EPITHALAMIUM FOR THE SEEDERS

Once there was a ruby-cheeked teenage girl
in brand-new Cuban heels, clicking through the cotton
patch to the justice of the peace to tie the knot
with her lanky, spit-shined beau, a few years her senior.
With a heifer and wood stove, they would thrive
at river's edge, churning butter, making clabber, and stoking fires.
They cut timber and sawed planks and drove nails
for the simple dwelling from which they would string
their story. They argued about whether seed potato cuttings
should have single or multiple eyes, about whose sprouts
would produce more potatoes to bank for winter.
But at day's end, he called her Rouge, and the river
serenaded them.

Now the old homeplace is in ruins, and mold beleaguers
the earth where the couple strawed and stored their food supply.
A single headstone marks their lives together,
as does the Bible chronicling their history. Amid the clippings
and clutter, their yellowing and stains, lie the scribbled names of
two sowers—the two from whose seed banks a bountiful crop,
offspring too many to number.

FAMILY REUNION

It began in the sixties the last Sunday in March under the old mulberry tree back home. A gathering of our clan. Eighteen children, whose Pa had settled the area from somewhere in or around Washington County.

They came from everywhere.

Aunts. The elderly ones with ear bobs like their big Buicks' headlights and with little black pocketbooks held fast to their bosoms, the aged, planting slobbery kisses to convey they were proud to see us, halting just long enough to tell us their troubles, adding, however, they had been doing the best they could. The middle-aged aunts, jovial, as stout as a pint of Guinness, sizing us up, lamenting that we had mended up or had fallen off, we, praying their summation would be the latter, having insured as much by eating our leafy greens and abstaining from our sweet tea a week or two before their evaluation. They were all star quality, particularly the one who had left home early to find her way in the big city, who had married up, who now sparkled her way into our world like an ice-kissed maple leaf.

Uncles. Male specimens akin to Clark Gable and John Wayne, leaning against the porch posts talking of the year's cotton and tobacco crops or laughing about growing up with Ma and Pa. Once in a while the conversation grew serious, moving to Normandy's beaches where one of them escaped certain death when granted unexpected family leave or shifting to the fallow field where the baby boy, returning from war, ended it all, leaving behind a beautiful wife full with child and potential. And there was the children's favorite who guaranteed his position by dropping a washtub of penny candy into their midst and then retreating to watch them scurry for Mary Janes and Tootsie Rolls and Fireballs and Dum-dums.

Today more ghosts assemble. We still spread a fine feast, still yak and laugh, still talk about what ails us. We still tell stories, full of hyperbole or down-right lies, and we still remove our hats before thanking God for His blessings and partaking of good rations. We still drink sweet tea, except lately some of the young folks are more concerned with sleek thighs than were their forebearers and thus abstain from our liquid gold. Over time we have introduced a few new practices, too. No gathering is complete nowadays without the perfectly roasted pig, its marble eyes and sleek black skin calling us to the table. And though we are confident we don't quite measure up to reunion days of old, we always give a nod to the spirits to welcome them home and to reassure them we're doing the best we can.

HOG BUTCHERING,

a communal rite of survival in late autumn's frigid temperatures
when men rise before dawn, fill washpots

with water, and light fires under them; when they dig a hole
to house a fifty-five-gallon drum positioned at a slant

for scalding and rolling the four-hundred-pound, squint-eyed
porker made still by expert marksman; when they hand-rake

to remove its bristles, expedited by turpentine in the boiling
water, then scrape its skin with long knives, razor-sharp

from the whetstone kept close at hand; when they string
the animal by its hind legs, eviscerating it from top to bottom

to extricate the parts like a skillfully-trained surgeon, laying aside
hams, shoulders, and side slabs, red-peppered

and Boraxed to ward off skipper flies in the smokehouse;
when they suspend the meat from the crib's ceiling joists,

smoke-drying it for a week or two; when women add
their expertise to the yearly ritual, grinding the fresh meat,

flavoring it with sage and other spices and then stuffing it
into scraped and cleaned casing to yield winter's staple;

when they pickle feet, tongue and trimmings in a vinegar
and spice brine to turn out head cheese or souse loaf to serve

alongside fresh fried tenderloin and tender buttermilk biscuits at
the noon-day spread; when in the afternoon men laugh

and hatch stories around a washpot seething with crunchy crack-
lings cooked in lard from the morning's meat processing

and then proceed to cut each other like felling a thirty-year long-
leaf pine or to brag about whose coon dog

could out-perform another's, whose cow would produce
the most milk. And so it goes every year when life slows

and nature delivers a cool snap—family flourishes, and cultural
and oral traditions survive,

at least for a while.

A PLACE OF CLEAR WATER

Variation on a Theme by Seamus Heaney

To go back to our place of clear water where teachers welcome
us with prayer and the Bible, the pledge and the light, and hugs
tight. Tight like shirt squeezed in Maytag wringer.

To wrestle with the 3 Rs, knowing we are destined for now,
for wooden desks aligned from A to Z, for long, wide windows
channeling our imaginations and the golden sun. To be

summoned by nod or yardstick to chalkboard, green; to crack
codes and solve problems, after which, privileged to pound eras-
er's white powder onto red brick, artists daubing our

canvases. Or to recite "Out, out, brief candle" or to diagram
dependent clauses or to practice our elocution. Like Cronkite
and Churchill and Cicero. To savor smells—hot, sticky

cinnamon buns, purple-inked ditto papers, and sawdust-cleaned
hardwood floors. To taste the cool, pristine liquid issuing forth
from the megalith fountain gracing the entrance the way a bride

adorns cathedral steps. To play dodge ball, baseball, hop scotch
and Red Rover and to be a Red Devil when the whole town
turns out to watch our Converse-shod basketball teams

"go, fight, win," even witnessing one of our own shatter fiberglass
backboard to stop the game, the next day headlining our state's
top sports stories. *The Adrian Animal Fetches*

an Extra Bowl of Cereal. To draw in our breaths like a syringe
extracting its vial's liquid when we climb the water tower
to leave our marks or when we scurry to duck and cover during

bomb simulations or when we line up, mouths open, to receive
pink-stained sugar cubes or to pox our arms or when we salute
our fallen leader in the autumn of '63, crushed by our nation's

hurt, hushed by its fears, unaware those moments
were soldered into our consciousness forever. To go back.
To our place of clear water. To see ourselves as we were.

To record our stories. Word after word after word.
That we might rein in time. That we might hold tomorrow
at bay.

A FAMILY CHRISTMAS

A hairy coconut with its three eyes
rolled in Daddy's hands
and hammered.
A trickle of juice
for a bevy of children
wide-eyed
salivating
hopeful
marveling
wide-eyed
glowing
anticipating
sparkling
wide-eyed.
A coconut, hairy
with three eyes
examined in a father's hands
and hammered.
A runnel of love to last
nine lifetimes.

THANKSGIVING

Every year it's the same, men waking before dawn in the crisp autumn weather to tramp through the woods, rifles and hounds in tow. For a few hours, they work up a hearty appetite for the noon feast, white specks already trailing the tiny kitchen like a comet's tail in the heavens as the matriarch sifts more flour into trough, creating a mountain from which she digs her well of lard and liquid. A magician, she works her hands to produce the perfect biscuit, tough enough to drag through homemade cane syrup and tender enough to crumble into pan for today's signature dish, cornmeal dressing, seasoned as perfectly as a pearl in an oyster shell. The bird, boiled tender into the night, rests, waiting to be drenched in the soupy bread mixture and baked to a golden brown.

And then comes chaos. Family descends like swarming locusts in Egyptian houses, and the queen mother ensnares her favorite son to sample the dressing to determine if it is fittin', a daughter to stir tea and check the peas, an in-law to pare apples for the salad to be finished off with Duke's and maraschinos, a cousin to cut a half-dozen cakes and pies and to spoon banana pudding. Nearby, a hefty voice expels children from the world of adults like he shoos chickens from the backdoor while other happy souls engage in laughter as hearty as the seven courses gracing the table.

Finally, the hunters arrive in lively fashion, discussing whose quiver held the most squirrels and who missed the most shots, a designated meat-carver makes art of the turkey, and a grand engages her granny in a lesson on burping a can of cranberry sauce. At length, we bow our heads to thank the Good Lord for His blessings, and without fail, a voice from across the room breaks the silence, "The biscuits, the biscuits. Don't burn the biscuits!"

SINGING THE BLUES

The Blues. Like rain falling softly on hydrangeas.
A longing. A sadness as weighty as scripture.
A bride's quiet sobs on her wedding night,
a mother's melancholy after her newborn,
a neighbor's fight with her not-so-true-blue husband.
Or your spat with a recalcitrant child. The heightened
tension. The plate on the kitchen floor, shards of glass
glinting in corners. The blows. The bruises.

Picasso, Elvis, and Robert Johnson felt the blues. I have.
Likely, you, too. When we plunge into despair and sell
our souls; when we're in our blue period, fashioning an old
guitarist, blind, poor, and as somber as church communion;
or when we put on our blue suede shoes and make soulful sounds
on street corners. In juke joints. In churches.
In solitary realms. When we gut the heart
and, like Louis A, spill out its recesses in song.

I'm so forlorn. Why was I born?
What did I do to be so black and blue?

Here's a story I heard once about convicts, conscripted
into public service to build roads and bridges, perusing
their surroundings for a way of escape; a guard, heavy
with tradition and self, watching the prisoners
like a pelican eying the ocean, rifle slung across
his shoulder, pistol, trigger-ready, on his side;
a kinsman, having trained dogs to hunt rabbits, to tree
coons, reasoning running the blood-thirsty hounds
to track his own children through the swamp would teach
the dogs to hunt a prisoner, jubilant when the convict
makes his escape, when the dogs are loosed on the trail,
when they follow the human scent down the river banks
through the soggy sloughs.

In the next scene at the foot of a tree
are the canines, mouths foaming like the sea;
on the ground, the crouched convict, hands covering
his head, as lifeless as Baal's prophets; the guard,
calling off the dogs, ordering the prisoner to his feet,
landing a punch with the heat of a July Fourth
celebration; the prisoner lunging forward, sputtering,
gurgling, withstanding kick after kick until the guard
is satisfied.

There's blood on the leaves and blood at the root.

That's the blues. They're raw. They keep us up at night.
They're conviction that demands action like—
like going down to the river to wash seven times
or penning another poem. Or two.

BLACKBERRY COOKING

For Mama
With Deference to Coleridge

In the mist, you're always there,
heavy with weight and wear, dipping
long-handled spoon into purple lava,
then lifting it above the pan's rim, tilting
it to inspect the juice's energy and flow.
At just the right moment, you lift pan
from stove's eye to cool the fruit before straining
it and pouring the warm liquid into a shining glass,
sealing with scalding Barr's lid. With a flourish
of dishrag to wipe away sticky residue
and with a tightening of band to secure lid,
you step back, satisfied, and wipe your hands
on your crimson-stained apron.

As the memory gels, steam haloing toward ceiling
and light dimming and shimmying across
lemony linoleum floor, I, too, step back, longing
for that other time, that other place, a place holy,
enchanting, for I've tasted of immortality,
and I've drunk the milk of Paradise.

DIGGING DEEP

Lessons on Beauty from My Mother,

who taught us to observe the Sabbath from sunup to sundown
to keep it Holy through rest and meditation. To make something
from nothing, to make do with what we have, like

gathering sagebrush for a broom, cleaning it and bundling it with
string or like drying Gallberry bushes, beating off their leaves to
make rakes for keeping the yard clean and inviting

for the bookoodles who drop by for weekend visits. To don
a pair of red shoes. To root roses and greet springtime
with baskets of coleus and ferns and bougainvilleas hanging

from the porch's rafters. To whip up a pudding in minutes,
a warm smooth cream with topping towering like winners'
morale, prompting second helpings and advice to dig deep

'cause the meringue is high. To powder the nose for funerals and
weddings. To wear a low bun. To make bi-annual treks
to the family cemetery to weed the plots and honor

the departed with plastic bouquets, chicory-yellows, rusty-reds
and cobalt-blues, arranged in jelly jars and coffee cans
and secured with stones at the head of the grave

finally meandering across the boneyard to ensure offspring learns
to respect the dead. *That's Cousin Sonny over there, and here's your
Grandma Vessie right here and little Susie Turner*

over yonder who died of the whooping cough in '45. She taught us
to care and not to care. To prop our feet. To put it in neutral.
To study robins and whippoorwills at twilight.

To welcome darkness after the dazzle of day.

THE KITCHEN

I dream of the kitchen at the back
of the house, a soft yellow with light
seeping in the tiny, corner window.
A kitchen with curtained shelves housing
Tupperware and ceramic bowls, thick-lipped;
mismatched, chipped plates and saucers;
a piece or two of cut glass from the S & H
Green Stamps store; and the stove, always
the warm stove, stained with the likes
of sugared and Sure-jelled blackberries, rolling
in their thickening juices that edge over
the dishpan's sides, making last attempts
at escape; the Mason jars sparkling
like infatuation on the Maytag; da Vinci's
Lord's Supper, over the washing machine
small, glassless, wooden-framed, the print
creased, splotchy, like Mama's hands.

UNDER THE BIG TOP

After Marc Chagall's Circus, 1964

In the bed of the '46 pickup
the family huddles like penguins
for the short distance
to the Greatest Show on Earth.
My face shows Entertainment a stranger in our world.
Already I smell the popcorn, the sawdust.
I feel the rush, imagining
lights and music and flawless feats.

We enter
the colorful menagerie.
The big top revealing
first the freak
and then the fat lady
and clowns cutting capers, shooting confetti
and exotic blankets adorning elephants, whose headdresses
and sequined girls dazzle the crowd gone wild.
And the gymnasts with poles displaying
versatility and balance.

We inhale and hold.

Confined to cages just moments ago, lions
now jump through fiery rings.
A trainer in ruffled shirt and white, stained gloves
lifts his baton.
On the drop, horses thunder past, and stunt men, practiced and
controlled, somersault
higher, higher,
on each other's shoulders.

Hang tight!
Trapeze artists
soar
spin
dive
defying the odds.
No safety net.

And unicyclists
perched three high
hands outstretched
circle—
one, two, three.

The greatest show on Earth,
well-defined and executed
tastes of death.
There's something—
something primitive about it.

I mean, the ring and all.

HOME,

a one-red light, one-police community where families slept with
open doors. Where mothers expressed little interest in Dr. Spock
and gave roaming rights to their kids to play Cowboys

and Indians, Tag, and Hide 'N Seek, at times to venture uptown
to mow a lawn for a little pocket change or on other days to get a
glimpse of the Goat Man crossing the state with his herd

and dilapidated trash wagon. A town of wrapped porches
with nobody taking advantage of them, of saw mills with wood
shavings carpeting the lumberyard like Midas' gold. A town

with a barber shop on Main Street, its rotating red, white
and blue cylinder and its King Edward cigar and Aqua Velva
tones inviting men to lather up for a shave and a shingle

and to converse about pick handles and governors or blueticks
and weather. With a pharmacy, its white-haired, white-coated,
druggist dispensing pills and concocting elixirs, his assistant

drawing fountain drinks and eavesdropping on young customers
sharing a two-strawed, cherry-coke-filled glass
and starry eyes. With Shell station across the street selling

penny candy, Baby Ruths, and Brown Mule tobacco
and prying caps off six-cent Royal Crowns if we agreed
to return the bottles, attendant scurrying like a squirrel

when a customer rolled up to the tanks, sounding the bell
for service––to pump gas, check oil and tires, wash windshields,
and speak neighborly, natural inclinations

for the grease-pocked worker. With a post office on the corner,
its masters doling out five-cent stamps, its first overseer distin-
guished at century's turn for having ascribed the town

its name. With a small, red-brick hospital, its dashing young
doctor and his beautiful bride serving the community well
but breaking when they buried their little girl, the result

of a vaccination he administered. With a restaurant
where, in the backroom, Al handled a que stick like Lancelot
taking up his sword. Where he plattered savory pit-barbecue

as if serving the last supper and offered a teen a job, enabling her
to purchase the console stereo for a home crying
for entertainment and to spin Sister Rosetta Tharpe

and The Blackwood Brothers on seventy-eights, occasionally
dropping Tom Jones and Neil Diamond on forty-fives. With an
Olympic-sized pool inviting youngsters from every block to

toast and tan. Except us whose faith barred near-naked bodies
and those whose skin excluded acceptance into the family.
With a park and benches overlooking Highway 80,

where the book mobile visited every other Friday, promoting
vicarious journeys into the worlds of Heathcliff and Catherine, of
Scarlett and Rhett. Into the deferred dreams of Langston

Hughes. With two grocery stores, Camels and Chesterfields
prominently displayed, along with white loaf bread as fresh
as a new perspective, where the bib-aproned butcher stood

ready to bundle up some neckbones or to cut a piece of ham,
even allowing credit for one's purchases, the running total
recorded on paper-sized, yellow ledgers at register's right.

With a furniture showroom that worked a deal for us to acquire
Pinkie and *The Blue Boy* to hang in our otherwise lackluster living
space. With Apollonian school where students shot spit

balls and lost their innocence and where teachers instructed
with love and passion and paddled with the same fervor
as they communicated the three Rs or planned field trips

on the *Nancy Hanks* to give us a glimpse of history. With
churches, the white frame one atop the hill to the south, the
stained-glass, brick edifice to the north, the rustic clapboard

structure in an area deemed the quarters, all three meeting
houses practicing their choirs for Easter services when parishio-
ners donned their finest from the dry goods store

which smelled of leather and antiquity and sprawled with shoe
boxes, bolts of fabric, Butterick patterns, dress zippers
and whose gentle proprietor waited on customers from the

shadows. Home. Where life gained traction or spun out
of control. Where dreams were realized. Or drowned. Where
time and chance left marks on the whole kit and caboodle.

LAMENTATIONS UPON
THE DEATH OF A NATION

Oh, it's a fine and useless enterprise trying to fix destiny.
—Barbara Kingsolver, The Poisonwood Bible

I was ten.

Wide-eyed, we stood at attention
before black and white television images,
but our hearts sagged like London's bridges.
The nation had just witnessed a riderless horse, a reversed
boot, a black-veiled widow with her children in blue.

Why has the young and beautiful fallen?
And in such a tragic way?
Was this his destiny? Did he sense it?
How about hers? Is it ours, too?
How will the kids spend Christmas? What will Santa gift them?
Will she smile again? Will we?
Why did the light go out at this moment? Is the new frontier still
an option?
Dare we skip rope, play hide and seek?
Will *ooo eee, ooo ah ah* become a dirge?
Will the nation crumble? How about our world?
Does the man in the moon cry now?
Surely heaven exists. Or is it like Camelot?

RACE TO WORK, 1968

At fifteen, I picked up my first job, just a mile away.
I dashed each day to the blinking lights of their diner.
Big shot owners wearing white, with a long, green Cadillac.
Their floors were spiffy clean. Money jingled
in their cash register, and I was caught in their world
like ball in pocket of backroom pool table. I served
barbecue and burgers and ice cream and fries
and put my dime in the jukebox to hear about painting it
black. Patrons left change on the counter, and I, quickening
my steps, swept it into my pockets, and jingled like wind chimes.
But then the others came, a window just for them
to order barbecue and burgers and ice cream and fries. I saw
their faces, and my steps slowed, and the coins no longer
jingled in my pockets.

SLAYING PRIDE

For James Kinney

It was during Monday's homeroom
in the business teacher's classroom
shortly after my father's hospitalization
when I was summoned to her desk.
"Your lunch has been paid for this week."
I swallowed hard, nodded an assent
and ambled back to my desk, positive
the world had overheard, sure my classmates
now aware of my poverty. For the first time
I saw my hand-me-downs, the too-long, woolen
skirt about my ankles, the rolled, white bobby
socks, elastic long gone, the thin cotton
sweater, misshapen, drooping from my shoulders
like a weeping willow. I gritted my teeth
to hold back the tears, to quell quivering
lips, and then folded behind the typewriter.
I felt the urge to pull the cover from the old
Underwood and begin the daily drill, to strike
the keys hard, to make words fly off the page
like sparks when flint and steel meet. *Now is
the time for all good men to come to the aid
of their country*. I remember not remembering
too much that happened the rest of the morning
except not eating lunch that day or the days
to follow. Couldn't swallow my pride.
Today, though, as I pen the memory, I focus
on another, a tender soul, the compassionate
teacher, reaching out to help his student, and
with fingers dancing across the keys
of my laptop, I dedicate this verse to him.

TAKING FLIGHT

In Memory of Mrs. Lawson

Mrs. Lawson opened each day with the roll call,
naming each of us with a smile, then placed her hand
over her heart to do her civic duty and to teach us ours.
At the chalkboard in her classic black skirt, cat-eyed glasses
and pumps, she taught us the art of diagramming
sentences, some clauses and phrases trailing the fence,
others peering from their pronged perches high above.
She entertained questions about space travel and took us
for a ride on the *Nancy Hanks,* and then drilled us
about our country. *The capital of Idaho is Boise, the capital
of Louisiana is Baton Rouge, the capital of Georgia
is Atlanta.* She taught us *thank you, yes ma'am* and *please,*
explained hormones and testosterone and a debilitating
sickness that leaves seventh graders starry-eyed and
weakens them like water weakens tea. After lunch
she recited *Annabel Lee,* dramatizing the winged seraphs
of heaven, inviting us to imagine, too, calling for words
to take flight, to dip and spiral, to dart and glide—in the air,
on the page, in our souls. When our classmate met
his untimely death in 1966, she allowed us to spill
our anguish onto the empty white page, then pulled us
all to her bosom as if she were stockpiling essentials
for a harsh winter, our sobs muffled in her purple,
rosemary-scented sweater, our slight frames sheltered,
secure. On that day, we comprehended the speech
of silence, and we understood the connotation of *wings.*

MIRACLE WORKER

For Mama Ruby

In her long-sleeved, aproned dress midway her calves,
her two long braids forming a bun anchored at neck's nape, she's
as beautiful and as rare as the pigeon-blood gemstone
from which she derives her name.

She labors hard chopping cotton,
laying off corn rows, feeding livestock,
then she treks back home to roll out biscuits,
fatback and love.

She works miracles as she powers through the day,
sweeping yard, heating wash pot, boiling clothes,
then silking corn, canning beans,
divining soap from lard and lye.

As she toils, she sings hymns about sowing and reaping.
Knowing the sins of the fathers are visited on the children,
she prays with a geyser's fervor and goes about her day.

In the evenings, she treadles the old Singer machine,
creating art from flour and feed sacks combed through
at the country store,
and understanding the potential of the widow's mite,
she scrimps for pennies
  to stow
into the palm of her college son.

Always, she knows her life's purpose—
nursing the sick, the lonely, the aged,
handing out mercy and truth and cups of cool water
in His name.

Ruby, unchanged by heat, reflecting light.
Ruby, a natural, full of brilliance, full of fire.

MEMENTO MORI

I was proud of my purchase on Mother's Day. Smiling
one of those rare small smiles that caused your eyes to dance like
bees, you hailed it the prettiest pocketbook you had ever

owned. A tapestry of purples, golds, garnets and blues swirling
with flowers and dragons and wizards and queens, its toasted
leather handles stitched sturdy, arcing like sun meeting sea.

Today it secures fragments of your life. A paper's torn
corner, the words "An empty grave" and "My Savior lives" vaguely
visible. Certificate for competency in basic life

support. Plastic comb. There's a folded white
handkerchief, a small black coin pouch securing hush money for
school lunches and the week's unexpected, your driver's

license, a major milestone at sixty. We laugh, recalling
moments you mustered the courage to sit behind the wheel.
The time in the watermelon patch you murdered a hundred

melons, nearly leveling us before we could stop the truck.
The time you plowed through the garden of our town's sole
police, killing boxwoods and azaleas and roses, almost toppling

the decades-old oak in front of the house. The time you earned
your first speeding ticket, the officer's frustration when you
informed him you would prefer not to sign the record.

The prettiest pocketbook you had ever owned. Our *Memento
Mori*. Not wilting roses or hourglasses or dripping candles
or stopped clocks. Not frayed photographs and torn letters

and legal documents and skulls. Just a purse that once made you
smile. A tapestry of purple, gold, garnet and blue reminding us of
the vanity of life. Of the certainty of death.
Of the futility of chasing the wind.

FOR YOUR GLORY

In Memory of Ruby

In 1976, I rebelled. I cut my hair. Perfect
timing, I reasoned. My sisters and I were to travel
to the Southwest with you, and they would help me lessen
the blow, for you adhered fast to your conviction
that a woman's tresses are her glory.

Anxious, I arose early to wash and style
my now wild and uncooperative hair.
I brushed and sprayed and parted and teased. Nothing
worked. Shocks sprang from my head like the Red Sea recoiling
to its banks. In a tizzy, I arrived at the airport
just in time to board the plane, rehearsing the defense
I would deliver you. But no speech. Not from me,
not from you. Just your acknowledgement of my sin.
You had such purty hair.

Years later you lie on the table, face and limbs hard
and cold in the warm, pulsating light. In silence
your daughters prepare you for your return to Mother
Earth, the youngest brushing your long silk
strands, glossy-black and silver-streaked, for what
seems an eternity, stroking it as if concerned
she will forget the feel, finally surrendering
the hallowed moment to the other who parts the hair
and meticulously plaits one side and then the other,
at last fusing two braids swathed at the nape
of your neck. With moves as deliberate and delicate
as spun glass, she crimps a tiny finger-wave
at your forehead and secures it with simple flat pins
the way you had planted them a lifetime.
The honor is complete. Sunbeams swaddle you,
and glory shines all around.

STRANGE FIRE

After Kristin Jónsdóttir's Washerwomen, 1931

Four fit Icelandic women
at nature's hot springs doing
what they do in a man's world.
A simple clothes-washing ritual
made as glorious as the dawn's alpenglow
by each other's presence, a simple work
from which come materials for other worlds
where Talent dictates tasks
and Imagination decrees duties.

Here, across the seas, our mothers, too, rising
early, fighting the cold, to draw water
from the creek, boiling, beating, blueing,
rinsing, squeezing, finally stringing
shirts and frocks, trousers and socks,
to dry on bushes and trees
or on lines stretched from post to post
in backyards and alleyways.
Like their sisters in faraway lands,
they fashion art with every beat
of the battling stick, pounding
away blemishes and wringing out
watery excesses, certain their work
judged by competitors, evaluated
by critics. With the stick's final flourish,
the women smile their shared secrets—masterpieces
sometimes come from everyday experiences,
and fire sparks fire when nurtured.

ELIJAH

My God is Jehovah

When I was a child, he seemed worn, but ageless,
tall, lanky, a bit stooped
in khaki trousers and khaki shirt buttoned to the top,
billfold snuggled in his breast pocket.
Partly bald, he often wore a hat,
sometimes felt and small, other times straw and large,
but always turned upwards on the sides.
His belt prong took in the last hole, the extra one, ice-picked,
and the belt's end drooped like a disciplined child.

He was the last of the mule farmers.
Tending a sixty-acre track,
he turned up the sod, fresh and cool,
as he plodded, brogan-shod, behind the two-horse plow,
often allowing the children to ride on the seat
he had rigged up on the cultivator.
In drought he prayed for rain but then walked worried
as he commanded the mules with his *gee* and *haw* and *whoa*,
taking pride in rows as straight as forthright talk.
One almost always sees him in the field
dusting the cotton to rid it of weevils,
shucking an ear of corn to inspect its maturity,
thumping the melon to check its ripeness.
Sometimes we see him placing his mail-order biddies
in the brooder, anticipating the Sunday delicacies
they would become or buying a mess of mullet
with the extra cash from the cotton seed,
even splurging on a lemon "sody" for himself
and on Neapolitan cream for the family.

He was our father,
protecting, instructing, correcting,
believing that a dose of Castor Oil would cure every ailment,
that swallowing Vicks Salve would cure the common cold,
that sparing the rod would spoil the child.
Like Vulcan, he awoke before day to start a fire,
stoking it with splinters from fat lighter stumps.
As the blaze roared, he would rub his calloused hands together,
satisfied that the house was waking to new life.

He was a man who had God's heart,
who commended his first-born to the Lord, bargaining
for His presence and a heavy allotment of the Holy Ghost.
In the middle of the night, he spoke in tongues
as mysterious and strange as the phoenix's rebirth,
sometimes dancing through the morning's early hours
on the creaking, wooden floors.

And then he was finished.
Sitting by the flame, legs purple and thin,
mouth as dry as the embers of the fire,
he blessed God's name and then passed the mantle
to his sons and daughters. Recognizing its power,
they rolled up the cloak and struck the water,
but when they asked for a double portion of his spirit,
the sea did not part for them,
and they did not cross the Jordan on dry ground.

A FATHER'S DAY STORY, 1939

I heard a story about family.
About how my father and his first-born
would trek the one mile
down the washed-out country road
to meet the school bus in winter.
About how her Shirley Temple curls
would freeze into place,
about how he would jimmy a cup
of tar from a bleeding pine tree,
lighting the gum resin with a long
red-tipped kitchen match to provide
heat for her frost-bitten hands.
I wasn't there, but I remember
smelling the pitch, his cupping
the flame, the black smoke spiraling
like happiness toward the heavens.
I remember the glow of the fire,
the warmth, the love.

CAMP MEETIN'

*All human nature vigorously resists grace because grace changes us
and the change is painful. —Flannery O'Connor*

It's mid-August. Funeral fans swish. Guitars hum.
Banjos and fiddles screech and whine.
But with good ears and vigilance, pickers tune and tighten,
and song bursts forth with a waterfall's force.
In the sweet by and by,
we shall meet on that beautiful shore.
In the sweet by and by,
we shall meet on that beautiful shore.

Then he moves in. With tar-pitch eyes
as penetrating as bullets, he scans
the crowd, and waving the Good Book as if conjuring
a spirit, he begins his diatribe on sin and the judgment
to come. Before long, his face reddens;
on his tiptoes with a volcano's fervor,
he thunders of hell's eternal fire,
of a burning sulfur, never consumed,
of God's wrath as destructive as a tsunami.
When the prophet pounds the podium and points
his crooked finger, chastising, condemning, shaming,
the place quakes with amens and hallelujahs.

Sometimes, though, judgment is immediate
as one moving from the fringes releases
a scream, interrupting the faithful like a sonic boom.
With flailing arms and sunken eyes, she speaks of dreams
and visions, prophesies of a death by water, another by fire,
the frenzy finally subsiding into fatigue and a hushed tone
as other women murmur, sway, moan and weep.
With hands clasped as tightly as a pendant holding a lock

of a loved one's hair and with forward gaze, they appear trance-
like, touched. And I am afraid.

Since then, decades have ambled towards forever,
sin's repercussions rushing our lives
like tidal waves. Today as the memory congeals
and the figures take shape, I, too, am touched.
There's a kind of fear that precedes faith,
an awe that comes with surrender.

THE STUFF OF DREAMS

For "W"

You were twelve, but you still recall, still feel
the rush of when you rounded the corner where you lived.

There he was, sidling down the street, the biggest kid in school.
When he walked, the earth shifted under his feet; when he

hurled insults, they echoed like a mudslide in the hollers.
"Hey, you. You red-headed, freckled-faced, four-eyed people

eater. I'll split your jaw." "Hey, you. You red-headed, freck-
led-faced, four-eyed people eater. I'll split your jaw."

You picked up the pace, vowing through pants and heaves to get
even, to take him on. Tomorrow. At track and field. You

would outjump him in the pole vault, outrun him in the 100-yard
dash, beat him at his own game. You were resolved,

as ready as a competitor bent for race. But he kept ambling
towards you. Satan in school-boy attire cursing, reviling,

antagonizing, goading like a parasite attached to host. And then
he swung. With the fury of a road chockful of potholes,

he bloodied your nose, spinning you into a frenzy the way infer-
nos spawn fire whirls, all the while laughing, pointing,

jeering, encouraging his cronies. Reeling, you pulled back,
instinct-driven, to even the score, but then, as if powered

by the Fates, you turned to walk the few paces home where you
buried your blood-soaked flannel shirt under the mattress

and stifled your sobs in pillows. In darkness when blood
cried out for revenge, you lost your love of school

and discarded your ambitions for track and field. That year
you failed seventh grade. That year you learned

the stuff of which dreams are made.

WITNESSES

December 2, 1973

i.
Awaiting ritual at church door
a daughter and a dad, her hand in his.
He renders a half-smile for the camera.

ii.
Five sisters in purple and gold velvet witnessing
a garter raised thigh high
the bride in lace and satin, beaming

iii.
a pastor, a groom, another dad
standing by for the moment to manhood
a certificate in prelate's hands, another witness

iv.
a tiny white-framed church, tapered with light
a white-and-gold framed Jesus in choir loft
observing amongst the lilies and ferns

v.
family and friends, a cloud of witnesses
their beehives and mini-skirts, platform shoes and wide ties
providing eclectic décor in traditional setting

vi.
Here comes the bride   stopping before altar
to whisper "I love you" to mother in blue knit
with purple-throated orchid at chin

vii.
At communion table, two vowing to love
till the poets run out of rhyme, until the twelfth of never
and that's a long, long time

viii.
Mints and nuts and petit fours
the couple, receiving blessings and hugs and slobbery kisses
bubbly, like the green-tinted sherbet punch

ix
A long, chromed Galaxy Ford carrying them into tomorrow
Going South to Get a Little Son, shoe-polished forever
into its blue and white finish

LAMENTATIONS OF THE CHATTAHOOCHEE

After Newspaper Account of Lynching Incident, 1913

It's a cool, crisp evening of spring, 1913.
A hush hovers heavy over the small Georgia town.
The people whisper.

When darkness falls, the sheriff and two deputies watch
the jail. All quiet. Until one hundred masked men
rush building with brushfire's intensity
and at gunpoint, order the law to work lock.

The black inmate is drug to the river bridge.
Lynched on the Chattahoochee's banks. Hung
from ancient oak. Riddled with shot.
There are rumblings of a blind tiger.

Townspeople lament the blot on escutcheon
and the death of their upstanding white citizen—
a young husband, a good-hearted boy
with strong family roots.

They impanel a jury to inquire about the hanging,
concluding straightaway death by strangulation.
By parties unknown.

It's a cool, crisp morning in spring, 1913.
There's a hush over the small, Georgia town.
The people whisper.

And the river cries.

HISTORY LESSON

I can feel the time closing in
I can feel the years crawling through my skin. —Elton John

It is a rare, cool, August morning
when we visit the old jail resting
beside the Chattahoochee River,
home to the county's rogues and misfits.
After archiving through time, we leave
the museum to walk along the river's
canopied birches, at times venturing
near the water to skip rocks and to hear
the river speak of its turbulent past,
to imagine willows' frank and forthright talk
about mobs, breakouts, thieves
and stolen kisses. Afterwards, we meander
through the quiet town searching
for the family home, smaller now and more
unmellowed than in your memory, at last
coming to the stiller town where headstones
also becry their past. At day's close, we stop
to catch our breaths. Through the café's
smoky window and the umbrellaed pedestrians
strolling along the square, I glimpse a likeness
of me, frail, scant, like leftover Christmas dinner.
For a moment, I archive my own history, its end
as lonely as the last ornament clinging
to the tree.

THE COUNTY FAIR

It's October. Sweater weather.
School has let out, and every student
has a ticket to the county fair. Excitement
is palpable as one hastens through sawdust
toward blinking lights and conglomerate
sounds—carousel's music, children's
squeals, donkeys' brays, and the hum
of gravity and death-defying mechanical forces.
The air electrifies like the sweaters' static.
Cloggers lift skirts and tip hats and tear out
on a reel, inviting the audience to clap or stomp
or slap their thighs. Exhibits show
quilters' and jam makers' accomplishments,
and rows of canned pickles display blue, red
and white ribbons, objects of pride
for students' hard work on the farm.
If folks follow their noses, they wind up in barns
where 4-H Club's prize goats and shoats
and calves mill about in hay, rooting, mooching,
pilfering. And the people scour around, too,
watching their fellow scavengers. Expecting
to win bouncy balls or pinwheels, kids pick up
rubber duckies circling in water, and teenage boys
throw darts at multi-colored balloons, praying
their marksmanship earns them oversized
teddy bears to hand over to their steadies.
Folks everywhere comb for corn dogs or cotton
candy or popcorn or elephant ears sprinkled
in powdery white. As people finish their eats,
workers invite them to step right up to side shows
to take in the world's greatest wonders—
the macabre, the bizarre, the strange.
There are knife throwers, sword and fire
swallowers, bearded women and snake handlers.

Here's a side note—a true story of a "freak"
captured on the banks of the Chattahoochee
in 1917. Heard County's sheriff turned him
over to federal authorities who invited Atlanta's
leading linguists to investigate the man's
origin and language. Phoneticians determined
the hairy creature spoke no language and
understood not one word, adding that though
he appeared harmless, they had no use for him.
Perplexed at how he and the county would
care for the man, the sheriff responded, "The
government doesn't want him. I don't want
him, and he won't run down rabbits, so what
am I going to do with him?" It turns out circus
and fairs from over the nation had learned of
the county's plight from Atlanta newspapers
and had a ready answer. They would use the
"freak of nature" for exhibition. But I digress—

As the sun disappears in the west, the fair's energy
revs up, and groups deliberate about the Ferris wheel
or zipper or bumper cars or roller-coaster, about
whether they will drop, suspend, hang, or fly. Screams
and bright lights hypnotize, and fair-goers hand over
their last tickets to greasy, hard-working, bandana-clad
workers and then belt themselves for the final thrill
of the evening.

The fair. Memories of yesterday. Of our youth.
Of our lust for life. But as we turn from that crisp,
autumn evening with its orange streaks
in the heavens, the chill is greater
than when we were school children. Perhaps
because today we no longer run rabbits
and few understand our language.

* The 1917 Chattahoochee account is archived at the Heard County
Museum in Franklin, Georgia.

EVICTION

For "W"

You've never gotten over it.
It's the same story year after year
like old movies at Christmas. I know
the scene by heart for I'm a student
of Ellison and you.

On the street, strewn from here to yonder,
an old army jacket and other pieces of clothing,
some still on hangers; a chrome and canary-yellow
dinette table and four chairs, next to which,
stained mattresses, a TV and its rabbit ears; a red
metal scooter, handlebar's shiny plastic streamers
still intact; travel trunk flipped on its side, dingy
newspaper accounts of war, letters, frayed, black
and white Kodaks spilling onto ground; nearby
an oversized family Bible, spine bent, pages
crumpled, hand-recorded birth and death
dates, clay-smeared; and the crocheted Christmas
angels, baby's blanket, shattered mirror
and broken dreams.

Every time you've recounted the story, I've imagined
the wind's howl and felt the cold's sting, blistering
like God in the whirlwind. I've seen you, slick-
haired, freckled-faced, big-eyed, and frantic, rummaging
with your Boxer through the scattered items in the ditch.
This time, though, as the story unfolds, we're both
on our knees searching, peeling back debris, looking
for the toy soldiers.

LIVIN' LIFE

The porch, life's center, allowing
for a little dab of religion
a right smart of politics
and a considerable amount of gossip
where tongues wag about schemers
and scandals, heroes and hellions.
"Good night a livin', did y'all hear-tell of that?"
and "Well, my goodness, I de-clare."

In daytime the porch refreshes
from field or housework and allows retreat
from summer storms, a chance to kick back
a minute and set a spell. Other times, the porch scurries
with pea shelling
bean snapping
corn shucking
and yarn spinning.
It's where neighbors assist one another
and throw up a hand to the passersby
as if to welcome them, too, where an ole coon dog rests,
one eye open, to spy on the fly invading his quiet.

At day's end when crickets chirp and fireflies mesmerize,
the porch turns as meditative as monuments
with men moving their thoughts toward tomorrow's field work,
how they'd have to get on the stick to make up for lost time,
how the weather would determine a failed or bumper crop.
As the men wheedle sticks and weave stories,
the young'uns lug mattresses to open air, praying
for a breeze to beat the heat; once in a blue moon, courtin'
takes place in the swing, and they steal a kiss or two.
Sometimes the porch extends to the country store
where old men play checkers and drink co-colers,
periodically sharing the brown bag for a snort, maybe more.

They pass judgment on their country, their neighbors, their kin,
but offer up remedies when Life deals blows or Death pays a visit.

The porch—
A place to raise a little cane, beat around the bush, or find out
what ails you.
A place that suits your fancy and blesses your heart.
A place of culture, community, and continuity where
dreams flower.

VERSE FOR SEAMUS HEANEY
AND MY SISTER

There's a favorite story about a lost slipper,
about a beloved poet retrieving it from the gutter,
inscribing verse on its inside, then returning
it. "You never know," he reasoned.

Shoes. They reveal secrets.
Dorothy's ruby-reds, Cinderella's glass
sparklers, ballet slippers, Converses, jungle boots
and galoshes. My sister's. Hers, an ugly, black
lace-up, heavy like conviction, attached to metal
leg brace, a memorial to life's losses.
And on closet floor, lined wall-to-wall like birds
on high wire, more shoes—pinks, blues, yellows,
slip-ons, lace-ups, leather and cloth, advocating
for her return to fit.

If time were yesterday, I, too, would pen poetry
for a shoe. For sneaker or loafer or Mary Jane or pump.
Or for the braced brogue resting beside her chair. With quill
and ink, I might slip into her sole and walk a mile or two.
You never know. You never know.

A FATHER'S RINGWORM TREATMENT, 1947

They were planets. The small, ring-like blotch
on my arm and the growing celestial body
on my head. Red flames, one inside the other,
garnering daily attention from every family member
and from the county's school and health officials.
But his was different. He pulled me close for inspection, carefully
surveilling the expanding orbit at the crown.
Then, like an astrophysicist studying mysterious
phenomena in the far reaches of space,
he separated a clump of hair and began removing
the single filaments from the waxing ball of fire.
I don't recall words or tears or pain. Just his eyes,
blue-gray orbs, determined but gentle; his hands,
warm, golden like the sun's beads of sweat,
as he poured the bottle of Listerine over my head
as if a libation to the gods.

INGENUITY

The spider
nature's mystery.
To leave home her first need
to escape the devouring of family.

Through her jeweled and silkened weave
she sends warnings and receives messages.
Her gossamer ensnares
her venom paralyzes.

Humans
like spiders
liquidate their kind—
if there is no communication or
retreat.

EPISTLE FOR SISTER

While He was in Bethany in the house of Simon the leper, as He sat at supper, a woman came with an alabaster jar of ointment, a very costly spikenard. She broke the jar and poured the ointment on His head. —Mark 14:3 MEV

The thrift shop I passed today
invoked yesterday's rituals
like silence welcomes morning.
I see you motoring through aisles
as tight as pressed wood plies, fondling
turtlenecks and scarves, smoothing
wrinkles, checking flaws. I watch you
examining the curves of every bone
china cup in store to determine
whether cracks and chips would warrant discard.
And how you loved shoes, purchasing the size ten
or the two because somebody somewhere
could benefit.

How I ache to hurry off
to one more pre-dawn garage sale with you.
To glimpse your eager face, to steady your gait,
to feel your spirit. To thank you
for pockmarked porcelain dolls,
for tea sets as tarnished as sin-ridden lives,
for broken clocks and worn-out threads.
For tattered cookbooks and dented tables,
faded pictures and love. Love like that
disguised each week in your five-dollar
bill arriving by college mail. If I could
reverse death's mortal coil, I would slip a note
into your palm to secure for you one more
sale, one more treasure, another pretty.
I would be that sister breaking

her alabaster spice box to anoint you
with extravagance, to bathe you in praise.

I would perform such a deed. A deed
about which our Lord need smile.
If I could.

FIRST BORN

Gently they go the beautiful, the tender, the kind...
I know. But I do not approve. And I am not resigned.
—Edna St. Vincent Millay

In '94, we celebrated her 60th birthday to thank her
for cementing our family. We shared about how she had given her
next-in-line sibling his first watch, a gift that had cost her several
days' wages;

how she had scraped a three-inch clearing in the windshield's ice
to drive neighborhood children to the two-room school where
she taught (but how she had nevertheless run over the Hoover-
carted man and his wife);

how Daddy had consecrated her to God at an early age and how
that knowledge had fashioned her being; how in winter she and
he had guided the mule-driven sled through the woods, collect-
ing resin from tin cups nailed to pines and how

she had taken vacation days to help him plant cotton; how Mama
and Daddy had sold a bull to send her to college but how she had
paid the gift forward for her eight younger siblings; how, in the
front porch swing, combing our long,

matted hair, she had imparted hygiene tips and allowed us to
rummage through her pocketbook to find red lipstick and quar-
ters and other foreign items and how she had pronounced "night"
and "sprite" in her signature drawl;

how she had never denied the brothers her new '63 Fairlane,
knowing that they, for a moment, would be somebody;
how, when we would sleep with her, our dreams were as light as
the morning mist because we knew she would keep out

the boogey-man; how she had acquired our pageant and prom dresses, even renting the gown in which one of us would be married and how she had whispered with her eyes she worshipped us.

Today we again celebrate family, holding an estate sale and extoling her person and position, but this time as we rummage through her belongings, we find loss heavy, heavy like citrons hiding in a picking of cotton.

BERLIN, 1945

After Dorothea

There's a story of yesterday as raw as winter winds.
As immediate as birth.

There were refugees from conquered cities reporting
women, children and the aged, like cattle herded
by day, their blood, doorposts-smeared by night.

There were raids. Always raids. Sirens. Hurried steps
to basement. Blackened windows and deepening wounds
and lengthening depression.

There was Mutti, a rope in each hand, making yet another
trip to cellar, visualizing soldiers, their onslaught
into city, their laughs, their jeers, their exploits

and celebrations; and with her, the little one in red coat asking
who and why and what if and when. There was talk of heaven. Of
Jesus. Of children snuggled in His arms.

There was the final descent into drafty darkness and then dawn,
its shadows revealing a scene as nightmarish as a Picasso.
Dangling from cellar's rafters, a long, limp female figure

like a blue ragdoll, and on the floor, a second rope, coiled
as if a serpent ready to strike. Outside a passerby shrugs
his shoulders and mutters, "It happens every day"

while the tiny figure in red plays in her sandbox, instructing
her paper dolls.

FLAKHELFER*

In Memory of Franz

I have heard fragments, how at fifteen, the Beast
conscripted your class into the air defense
of his lair, how you admired the Allies' tight formation
over your capital city, their bravery in the hail
of shrapnel, how you collected metal,
war's trappings, your souvenirs.

I heard how you and your comrades strayed
from your squadron, how, in fear-thick air,
your heart constricted when you eyed the enemy,
how they bandaged your wounds, and at war's end,
released you with directions home. I see you
legs as swollen and heavy as water balloons,
holding fast to survival, arriving to discover
a mother's self-immolation, sisters' hard faces
and rubble.

I learned how guilt through the years had suffocated
you like an umbilical cord strangling a newborn,
how you wrestled with your complicity in nations' atrocities,
and how at St. Michael's, where the Beast's Moonlight
Sonata had unleashed decades-deep destruction,**
you experienced your own blitz, emerging
from the cathedral's ruins a new creation with a faith
as strong as war's rhetoric, having acknowledged
man's propensity for evil.

Sometimes I look at your time-ravaged frame and consider
how determined Memory is, directing mortar shells
and flares to disturb night's rest, displaying tanks
and air power as day dawns, reeling the horror
like a newly-discovered black-and-white film. But on this day
as light advances, you hear another *Moonlight Sonata*.

You jump and turn and dart and glide to the master's
baton. You're a child. Home once more. *Quasi
una fantasia.*

*Soldier; Hitler's youth
**Operation Moonlight Sonata: The name of the Nazi military
operation which pounded Coventry, England, in November 1940

YESTERDAY

In Memory of Frank

The past is never dead; it is not even past. — *William Faulkner*

There he stands in his wingtips, white bibbed-apron around his waist, dropping corn-mealed catfish into the seething oil. He has a knack for it. The barn behind speaks of him. Rusted horseshoes, kerosene-filled lanterns and an old ice-house pick adorn the outside as do mule halters, hog tusks, turkey beards and feet. The walls inside take on deer heads and cotton weights, fish nets and poles. Beside the outhouse built to symbolize his youth are a grape vineyard as lush as those of Eden and pens readying wild hogs for the freezer. It's the dog days of summer, and sweat beads on his forehead like diamonds, a reminder of his time behind a two-mule plow, yet another item taking up its rightful space in the shelter. He is a son of the soil, always enjoying the fruits of his labor. Contentment for him is sitting on the screened porch, wash pan in his lap, shelling purple hulls gathered from his own garden in the early morning dew or it's easing down the river in his Jon boat in late afternoon, checking fish baskets secured at water's edge. I imagine him talking to God, thanking Him for His beauty and bounty or thinking about the Bible story he fondly told to anyone who would listen. About how, after Christ's death, the dejected Peter told his friends he was returning to his old profession. "I go a fishin." About how Christ had appeared on the shore and had built a fire. To cook fish for His friends. To show His love.

The sun is directly overhead now. I see fish piled as high as Mount Ararat on the platter, so high, in fact, brim and catfish spill over onto the red-checkered tablecloth. I smell hushpuppies. I see him hang the tongs on the grease pot and slip his apron over his head.

He had a knack for it.

BROTHER PROPHET

Our bones are dry, our hope is lost, and we ourselves are cut off.
—Ezekial 37:11

A drought has settled
upon our little plot of wilderness
since you left us.
The land is scorched, the branch
empty, corn rattles like diamondback
in field, and we're as hollow as a rotted stump
since you have been gone.
Where are your stories? Your songs?
Is your witness buried, too?
How can we share bread with family to break barriers
if you are not here to build the fire? How do we arbitrate
community disputes with our parched tongues
if you are not the appointed judge?
We're living in the valley of brittle bones.
The well is dry. We need you here
to speak truth, to irrigate our thirsty souls
to reconstruct us bone-by-bone
and cover us with new skin.

PSALM OF LAMENT WITH PHRASE FROM GERARD MANLEY HOPKINS

In Memory of Tina

Today I water
the Christmas cactus
left on window's sill,
its drooping purple bloomers
clustering like bells to toll your death
one more time. You, snatched,
without warning. How my soul
languishes, languishes like the ledge's
smooth, leathery desert flower.
Oh thou lord of life, send my roots rain.

CATS AND DOGS

In Memory of Carl

In the winter of '19, it rained
like a cloud of bats emerging at dusk
from their dark cave. After clinging
to ceilings or walls or rafters.
After grooming themselves
for nocturnal exploits. It rained
like politicians' hot rhetoric, like their punches
landing smack dab middle of the gut
or between the eyes or in heart's coeur, the talk
of collusions and invasions and conspiracies,
spew and vomit drowning nations. It rained
like the spread of Cogongrass in spring,
its white flowers arranged as silver cylinders,
its rhizomes long and scaly and sharp.
It rained like a belching fire, like the solitary figure
of Hopper's paintings, the lonely road, pensive
evenings at nightfall. Like gray.

CONSUMMATION

And when thy loss shall be repaid with gains
Look to my little babes, my dear remains.
— Anne Bradstreet, "Before the Birth of One of Her Children"

The weekend before your June birthday
we shuffle through an old trunk's legacy.
A lot of deaths of late and memories
as severe as a violin's broken string.

Pictures show your father "the blue-eyed Brando"
posing with old flames to steal kisses and seal fates.
Valentines and love notes spark smiles as does her
letter confirming a meeting at the crossroads
when he returns from war.

There's a hospital invoice dated June '51
for room and board, medications and fluids,
plasma and blood. Across the front, his signature
with inscription, "Paid in Full."

And the tiny box

from which we uncover tiny, leather shoes
with markings like chocolate-marbled milk
and baby book with nothing penned.
No note, no record, no
nothing.

Haltingly, we close the trunk and linger,
imagining one more meeting at the cross-
roads of another Time and Space.

BREATHLESS

Life's greatest happiness is to be convinced we are loved.
—Victor Hugo, Les Miserables, 1862

It was the summer of '73.
You had me at hello.
Unlocking your office at the student center,
you commanded space—even then
I knew you would take care of things.
And me.
And you did, immediately
replacing my beat-up Beetle's bald tires and bad breaks.
Lanky then, your hair as red as Dorothy's slippers,
and shoulder-length, and your long-lashed eyes hinting
of our tomorrows, you wooed me with your mustached
smile, roses and James Bond.
We picnicked and soaked up summer's rays
and tricked the sun.

That year was full of beginnings—
my first glimpse of the ocean as expansive as Time
(It left me breathless or was it you?)
a sick father whom you cradled in your arms
like an orchid's petal enfolding its lip.

So much to love
the snuggling, bodies as entangled as fishnet
the rituals—Saturday morning sleep-ins, the late autumn boat
rides, the artist in you
(If you were a landscape, you'd be grasslands, adaptive,
open, vast)
your songs and ditties
your tolerance of Shakespeare
your work ethic
your quick wit
your passion for old cars and God
your devotion to children
that you can do anything and will—
except Time has hit the foot feet
and you can't stop the acceleration.

A WEDDING BLESSING FOR OUR DAUGHTER

After Jane Hirshfield

Today when the ocean is emptied of
 sailboats and fishing rigs
 and white sands serve up oil
 like scalded flecks of flan

today when rain falls
 like silver confetti
 after the monsoon that sat days
 like an unclaimed postal package

today when your daddy prays
 for a dove beaking a tender olive leaf as a sign
 of receding waters and then buckets away
 brackishness that his little girl might take her vows, worry
 furrowing his face like melted snow chiseling
 mountains

today when we cross
 the small-boats marina under clear-colored umbrellas
 sheltering your wedding cake, the cake you crafted
 with a favorite cousin and four dime-store mixers
 making laughter to linger a lifetime

today when we lunch
 one last time as a threesome
 taking in sanctity of sea
 and moment

today when we witness
 a world where musicians play and godmothers wave
 wands, where you draw a deep breath and then round the
 corner to behold your prince, your smile exploding like a
 million constellations

today when you descend the stairs
 on your daddy's arm, beautiful in cream-colored, Grace
 Kelly gown and milky-pearl bracelets and strappy, diamond-
 studded slippers, radiant
 like crystal under fairy lights

today when you stand
 before the lily-clad altar with him to start your new life
 minster blessing, friends and family cheering,
 a special brother interjecting, "I give her, too"

today when we feast
 on lagniappe and wedding cake and delight
 in candle-lit spheres ribboning from boughs
 like rainbow bubbles and in the penned bottle messages
 you will unseal the first anniversary of this occasion

today when we toast
 to your happiness and dance under stars peeking from the
 heavens and sparkle you with love on your way
 to the limousine that will whisk you away
 to his kingdom,

 let the memory with its rain-scented softness
 and rose-tinged longing seal you and him forever.
 Amen.

ACQUAINTED WITH GRIEF

It was January when you called.
Sadness blanketed you in gauzy gray.
I lost the baby. A hush ran the phone line
like water colors. I—I had not surmised
you were with child. What does a mother do?
What does she say? How does she ease the pain?
And then as if in full throes of labor, you deliver
the words, *A drop of hot oil blotched my wrist*
this morning. I hope it scars. I don't even know
if it were a boy or girl. Cribbed into the psyche
forever. Like milky waterfall cascading over cliff.
Like delicate, haunting sounds of carousel.

SWIMMING LESSON

It is a late June lesson. The sky threatens.
And so do five-year-olds. Sobs, cries, all-out wails.
Fear as palpable as the muggy, noon-day heat.
The instructor, like a merciless summer heat wave, calls
you to the deep. *Chin down! Arms out front! Like Superman!*
Don't fight it! You edge forward, shivering, shoulders as hunched
as grackles' wings. *You can do this! The water is strong and will*
hold you up. Glue-footed you are. Tentative. Panic painting your
tiny frame. *Jump! Now! Right now! I said now!* You fill your lungs
and lunge, breaking the water, stroking toward her as if every
drag might be your last. *Breathe! Pull! Kick! Breathe!* She offers
her hand, then shoves you toward the shallow where you emerge
for her high-fives and atta boys. *See, you have swum the pool's*
length. Lips quivering and eyes tear-filled, you inch out of the
water, cutting a glance at your mother. All you see is her pride.
What you don't detect are muffled whimpers escaping her
very core. A heart flutter-kicking. How well she understands
water to be strong, dear son, so strong, in fact, it can bear you
up. But she knows it to grow dark and billowing and treacherous
and wild. She prays for lifelines, our precious one. She pleads for
buoys.

LULLABY AT DAWN

For "C"

I remember it was your college years,
a weekend at home, and you were sleeping
in. An act of mutiny for your grandmother
who had raised nine children
during the Great Depression and the war
years and who had never slept past sunup
in the nine decades of her life. She simply
could not contain herself. *Now that one*
don't do nothin'.

Today in this global pandemic, I see
you working the night shift,
your big brown eyes behind shield
and N-95, and I swell with pride. I hear
your stories from the ICU, about another
granddaughter Facetiming you to help
her say goodbye to her beloved matriarch,
your sobs and chest heaves clouding
the plexiglass masque like steam rising
from a body of water after a summer rain;
about a coworker holding her sibling's hand
every day, exhorting him to return to life;
about the young nursing student with whom
you feel a special affinity, rallying
when iron lung and human spirit and the Divine
mesh for a miracle.

And for the record, my daughter, as Aurora
signals the end of yet one more long night,
I suggest there are other kin beaming
and bragging and swelling with pride.
If you close your eyes and lean in quietly,
you might hear the aged one humming
"Brahms' Lullaby" from across the Milky Way.
I bet she is whispering, *Sweet dreams.*

HOW TO LIVE

After Pablo Neruda, Wendell Berry and Dylan Thomas

Live now. Redefine "one day" and "perhaps." Prepare to fly
through galaxies and eons of stars. That blaze and burn

and burst. Take washtubs of pictures to seal life's real moments.
Dissect more flowers and plant more

dogwoods—crosses are important. Grow a vegetable garden.
With sunflowers. Sow beauty. Don't saunter between stop

signs. Race between them. Start writing poetry early. Perfect it
akin to Gerard Manley Hopkins and Seamus Heaney. Paint

over the green eyes of envy and splash them with softness. Like
blush. Or rose. Unravel all unkind word strands spoken

to and about family. Shy away from timid hugs, and show more
love, less distance. Look people in the eye and listen,

really listen; make them feel visible. Know that when hair loss
and other physical changes steal self, God's love and others'

change the way you look at you. (My daughter reminds me my
style demands big hats and bold scarves.) Don't be too vain.

Too materialistic. Too stuck on self. Walk in the infirms' braces
and speak their language and take on their smiles. Fight

for injustice, and be one to the infinite power. Sleep
with your mother during her last weeks. Those times

are as sacred as Byzantine art. Walk humbly with your God, invit-
ing Him to open and close doors; learn to see problems

as His opportunities and to revel in the thought that when you
are weak, He is strong. You don't have to understand why

the rain falls on the just and the unjust; just know that God is
God. Talk with Him. Often. Copy your daughter's zest for life

and accumulate myriads more memories with her to stamp on
the annals of your heart. Catch lightning bugs with the grands.

Carve pumpkins for them. Have sleepovers and pillow fights. Act
silly. Listen to the rain on a tin roof, and view more sunsets

on the water. Hold hands with your spouse every day, snuggle to
share his breath. Above all, choose kindness,

and when your time comes, do go gentle into that good night.

POST HOC LESSON FROM MAINE, 2019

If Adam and Eve had not introduced sin into the Garden of Eden,
if man were not preoccupied with slaughter since Cain

and Abel, if the war to end all wars had not been underway, the
Allies desperate, the U.S. shipping munitions to France, if

the *Mont Blanc* had not stopped in New York and loaded six mil-
lion pounds of TNT and picric acid to destroy

the Germans, if regulations had not been relaxed, if the cargo
ship had not navigated through a narrow harbor toward the

Halifax piers, meeting the *Imo* approaching from the opposite
direction, if one had not been pressed to get in, the other

determined to get out, if the two ships had blasted their whistles
more often, if the *Imo*, a Norwegian freighter, had not

defied navigation conventions, passing ships on its left again and
again, if it had not reversed its engines at the last

minute, swinging its bow and clipping the bomb-carrying vessel
at the forward hold, sparks igniting—small decisions,

incalculable results—if there had been warnings of the explo-
sives, markings on the rig, if the crew had not abandoned

the burning ship, if they had spoken English, if it were not rush
hour, Halifax buzzing with life—kids going to school, pockets

filled with combs, marbles and hand-whittled pencils, business-
men ambling to the office, factory workers clocking in,

all stopping to watch the burning ghost ship drifting toward Pier
Six, all intrigued by intermittent fireworks in the morning sky, all

pointing and shouting, oohing, and aahing until the fire reaches
the main cargo, if the blast had not blown windows

inward, blinding residents by the hundreds, if kerosene lanterns
had not overturned, fires had not started, if people had not been

trapped, if the explosion had not caused a tsunami creating a
thirty-five-foot tidal wave that sucked men, women and

children into the harbor, drowning them in its wake, if the bliz-
zard, bitter and vile, had not blown in, leaving the sick,

the sightless, the homeless in make-do housing, the dead in
make-shift morgues, if the town clock had not stopped.

On December 6, 1917, at 9:05 A.M.

STRANGE FIRE II

We fool with fire, we get burned. Perhaps
we even burn in hell. In Milton's sulfurous fire.
In those darting flames that don't die. But we play
anyway, burning candles at both ends, addressing
burning bushes, occasionally setting fire to rain. We
fire rockets, canons, tear gas, and hate, learning
early that fire is the devil's only friend. We burn
calories, coal and countries while we watch meteors
burning in the heavens, oil burning in the Gulf and money
burning in our pockets. Our muscles burn, our ovaries
and our eyes, and we burn, burn, burn with desire, falling
headfirst into its blazing ring. We fool with fire,
we get burned. Ask Nadab and Abihu, Uzziah and Elijah.
Ask Lot's wife.

I AM

In Memory of Jason

I am a sensitive, easy-going girl who loves sunsets.
I wonder why the grass is green and the sky is blue.
I hear the bright, yellow stars bursting in the sky.
I see the beautiful light of the midnight moon.
I want to live my life to the fullest, making every day count.
I am a sensitive, easy-going girl who loves sunsets.

I pretend that everything is as it should be, no crying children
  or loneliness among the used.
I feel that everyone is here for a purpose.
I touch the tradition of Christmas, Thanksgiving and the love
  of kin.
I worry that life is too short.
I cry for those who worry about the afterlife.
I am a sensitive, easy-going girl who loves sunsets.

I understand the pain of leaving friends and losing family.
I say that everyone chooses to be happy.
I dream of a world that's all family.
I try to understand everyone's point of view.
I hope that everyone can feel the urgency to be an organ donor.
I am a sensitive, easy-going girl who loves sunsets.

Cortney Taylor Wade
Age 13

A PRAYER FOR MERCY

Be merciful to those who doubt. —Jude 22

It was a special gift. A family heirloom
wrapped in tinsel tissue ribboned
in bold, a silver serving spoon,
its ladle etched with gratitude.
Thank you for feeding our son.
Unique. Well-thought-out. Priceless.
A treasure for all my days.

But now, years later, the gift stops
me cold like a blue norther.
Did the teacher in me offer hope
or despair?
Did she encourage
or tear down?
Did she miss opportunities
or make them?
Did she feed her sheep?

Oh, God, be merciful. I need a do-over.

PAEAN FOR THE CREATOR

Oh, Lord, our Lord, how majestic is thy name in all the earth.
—Psalm 8:1

Praise Him at dusk and morning and at times throughout
    the day
For wetland's crickets, reeds and bullfrogs, their songs
    and melody
For oceans lapping, the stars' silence, for babbling brooks
    and white moonlight
For waters roaring, rising, cresting, cascading from grave
    heights

Praise Him for splendid sightings, the strange, average,
    the small
For the mighty eagle mounting skyward, red-tailed hawk, its
    scream, its call
For the wounded, fallen sparrow to whom He gives much love
    and thought
For the butterfly, its flight slow sailing, for worm and bug His
    hands have wrought

Praise Him for every creature crossing paths of roaring seas
For dolphins bubbling, surfing, jumping, playing tag and with
    great ease
For starfish and the jelly, the white whale, the slug, the shark
For hermit crabs that scuttle sideways, for oysters, snails, that
    leave their marks.

Praise Him, you throng of people, you children everywhere
With a loud voice and jubilation, show our God how much we
    care
If we fail in exultation, if we let our chance pass by
Rocks will cry out, nature will shout, their voices raised sky high.

EXPOSED

I marvel at the egret, her charm and elegance,
her pristine plumage as white as moonlight, and daring.
At her long, jet-black legs slippered in chicory as she moves
serenely and elegantly along banks, peering intently,
eyeing little fishes in the shallows. She's subdued, patient,
foraging the waterfront by foot, stirring pools and eddies
as she drifts. Sometimes she flies just above
water's waves. Other times she swims or glides and dips.
This morning she's restrained and poised, still, like
hurricane's eye, awaiting her prey. And then she swoops.
With dexterity and grace, she dazzles and awes,
and I am exposed. Exposed to the grandeur of God.

REVELATION

After Winslow Homer's Perils of the Sea, 1888

Behold, I am insignificant; what can I reply to Thee?
I lay my hand on my mouth. —Job 40:4

From the ship's stern, I hear God's undulating voice
see Him in all his majesty and power
in all His creative force
in all His manifold presence
as He stretches out his hand
to gather the waters in a heap
to send them forth, willing them to stand fast, to heed
their boundaries. The dark blue waters
spraying, crescendoing, cresting,
foaming, frothing, billowing,
raging. A reminder that a moment is
as fragile as a bubble released from its wand
that man washes away even as he builds fleets
to navigate the turbulence
and to manifest his own worth.
Yet the waters like crystals entice, inviting
Leviathan to play there
dolphins to cavort
man to meditate on The Almighty's sea-sculpted caves
to consider His wonders
and the deep to proclaim His glory
His intent to judge the world.
But man, nestled in his hubris, heeds not Nature's counsel
until the waters increase and the light alters
and the winds lay siege to his certainty.

PANTOUM FOR GOOD FRIDAY

Nature weeps, it's the darkest and strangest of days,
    His blood is now on man's hands,
The Christ who hung the galaxies in space,
    Who numbered grains of white sea sand.

His blood is now on man's hands.
    They crown Him with many-a-thorn,
Who numbered grains of white sea sand.
    They mock, spit and scourge, and they scorn.

They crown Him with many-a-thorn
    and nail him to rough-hewn tree.
They spit on, mock and scourge, and they scorn
    while the thief cries, "Remember, Lord, me."

They spit on, mock and scourge, and they scorn
    The Christ who hung the galaxies in space.
While the thief cries, "Remember, Lord, me,"
    Nature weeps, it's the darkest of days.

THE MORROW PERHAPS COMES WHEN

rain drowns deserts and seas
and the nightingale quits her rich song
when winter spills over into springtime
and we build solidarity with the cold
when grass empties green into the earth
when breath plays Hide-And-Seek
with our lungs.

But if the morrow should come
when the winter extends to the spring
it is then the stars gather to praise
man's spirit, undying, always.

JUDAS

After Carl Bloch's The Last Supper, late 1800s

Traitor, hypocrite, informant, fraud,
confined to Hell's Ninth Circle,
a reminder the heart is deceitful above all else
and desperately wicked.

Your name suggests a dad
well-versed in Holy texts,
a mother's hope for her son.
You were the South's sole disciple,
isolated from the start,

yet enraptured
by His love, His parables, His feats,
perhaps performing miracles yourself—
the lame would walk, the mute would talk,
and the dead would burst forth from their graves.

But afterwards you became disillusioned;
your heart hardened like the aspen wood
on which He would be nailed.
You could not grasp
He would not saddle a white horse for conquest

but would save the world through surrender
on Golgotha's Hill.

Alas, you negotiated a deal, struck a bargain,
and with kisses you sold your soul and the Savior
for thirty pieces of silver, a price foretold.
Then with blood on your hands, you discarded
the shekels in the temple and hung
yourself on a tree, a fitting reminder
your sins would find you out.

Judas, you walked with God and knew
what could have been.
Now your bones dry in Potter's Field
to await the final judgment,
and we honor you
in the tradition of Cain.

ABSALOM

After David Reznick's David's Lament for Absalom

Oh, Absalom, Absalom,
beautiful Absalom,
announced by a throng of runners,
a chariot's spectacle.
From crown to sandals, no defect.
And your hair, your hair, weighed like revenge.

Your charm was your decoy,
your charisma, a magnet for the young.
Kissing their feet, you hid your agenda
and stole their hearts.
They made you king, realizing not
your treachery manifested itself
in arson
in murder
in lies.

But pride goes before a fall.

You chanced upon your enemy.
Seeking escape,
you caught your locks in the forest's terebinth.
Unhorsed, you dangled
like a broken bough
until your heart was lanced, your body beaten.
They threw you into a shallow place,
stones, a scant pile,
to mark your grave.

Oh Absalom, Absalom!
How dangerous to sow strife
to root bitterness
to erect monuments to
Self.
Would to God your legacy were written in water,
not on your father's heart.

APOSTROPHE TO DAVID

Beautiful boy, we feel your taut, sinewy muscles as you poise
yourself, rock-ready to fell giant and nervousness.
We surmise that Goliath, distracted by your fine physique, lost
his life before Philistine hosts, that Bathsheba, lured
by your charisma like ladybugs drawn to sunshine,
undressed herself on the rooftop. And Saul, who summoned
you to play the harp—did he grow jealous and melancholy
as his eyes met yours? Even the Almighty fell for you,
handpicking you king, deeming you a man after His own heart.

Oh, mighty one in stone! We've defended you as gentle
shepherd, poet-musician, prophet-priest pointing to another
chosen. Even after relationships as fragile as robins' eggs,
you were still The David. Paragon of virtue. Larger than life.
Of mythic stature.

But is art reality? Beauty, truth?
For when you were stricken with years, you could
not constrain the cold, despite the many blankets.

SALOME

After Henri Regnault's Salome, 1870

After two thousand years you still dazzle.
Here you are on canvas, sultry, rosy-cheeked,
shimmering in gauze golds, your dark tresses,
shadowed face and half-smile as mysterious
and beguiling as the gem-eyed serpent bracelet coiled
about your upper arm. With one hand on hip,
the other resting on ivory-hefted knife sheathed
in red, you tout danger, a readiness to pounce,
a willingness to do the dirty work. You pose,
poised for power, as wild and barbarous
as Dionysian fertility rites.

Over the ages you have intrigued us.
We have taken to art to depict your charm,
your sparkle, our fascination like the pull
of north and south magnetic fields. We have
dramatized how you seduced the leading
men of Galilee with dance, how Herod Antipas,
frenzied with wine and wantonness, offered you
half his kingdom, how you demanded
more; you, bent on blood.

Could we be deceived? Might
you have been simply the lioness' cub, a damsel
distressed, the pawn moved on the chessboard
by a cold, calculating, grudge-holding mother?
Were you caught in a snare like a moth
in a spider's web when you called
for the prophet's head upon the platter?

Oh, but no matter, Salome.
Violent delights have violent ends.
Death at last stalked you to a frozen river
and cracked the ice.

SONNET IN THE TIME OF COVID-19

How terrible the need for God. —Theodore Roethke

We did not see it coming, so we say,
We mask ourselves, we hide, else we're consumed.
We know not what to do but cover face,
The virus like a jackal signals doom.
Our lives are shaken, we bear pain, bear loss,
Millions of souls languish without a cure.
Baffled, doubtful, confused, we sign the cross,
The days are dark, our future seems unsure.
Yet we hold fast, we don't give up or cave,
The God who helped us in our past still lives.
Our breath, our strength, our hope, He longs to save,
He soothes our hurts, our fears, so much He gives.
So live, hold high His banner, shield, His rod,
Stand still and see the salvation of God.

RED BLUFF, 2020

It was a bizarre place to share
a Thanksgiving meal—off the old Red Bluff Road,
past the little red-brick church atop the hill, then down
the dirt path along the barbed-wire fence, over which
lay discarded artificial roses and broken pots and dreams.

                                        In silence,
we arranged poinsettias on the pebbles enclosed
in granite coping, careful not to disturb the peace,
and arranged our chairs to ward off November winds
moving across the open field like an ostrich on the
savanna. Hungry from early-morning preparations
and the several-hundred-miles to get to this sacred spot,
we spread across the tailgate the tubs of fried chicken,
the mayonnaise-slathered pineapple sandwiches,
the paprika-dotted deviled eggs, and then added potato
pies and pecan pies, golden in mid-day sun.

We spoke of COVID, the election, our forebearers resting
at our feet. We acknowledged our year's shortcomings
to the pines, the spirits and each other, and vowed life
changes that would grow legacies left latent heretofore
in this boneyard. We offered up poems and gave gifts
and strolled amongst the dead, calling out names
and speculating on lives edited in etchings and epitaphs,
markings and dates.

Then we gathered our things and held there
        another minute,

glancing one more time at the hallowed ground,
the dust to which we will soon return, the dirt
that will house our own bones.

THE BEST IS YET TO COME

After Lorette C. Luzajic's The Best Is Yet To Come and After Muhammad Ali

We live in chaos. In the arena's blinding lights and deafening
noise. Hypnotic dreams *float*ing like butterflies, *sting*ing
like bees. We're on the ropes with trainers pummeling
final instructions, managers clouting money,
the crowd's passion, red like slaughter.

Then the bout begins. Pivots and bounces and crosses and jabs.
We're swaying like a punching bag suspended in the gym's corner,
as disoriented as a sparrow glancing off glass. A dip and a cut and
a Strike! And a Bam! One, two, three, we're out
for the count. Until—

Until the Great Champion, the Pride of Jacob, lifts us
to our feet and raises our arms in triumph, proclaiming all
things new. No death, no dark, no curse, no pain. Victors.
For eternity. Reigning forever and ever.

I LEARNED THIS YEAR

that oodles of black-widow spiders can hatch
from one grape-sized sac, perhaps as many as
seven hundred

that the 27th president, William Taft, kept a dairy
cow named Pauline on the White House lawn

that the world can shift while you take a breath
or not

that Dante Gabriel Rossetti fixated on the poetry
manuscript he placed in the coffin of his muse and then
devised a plan to exhume it under the shroud of night

that mama tigers make a purr-like sound,
a chuff, to comfort their cubs

through the wisdom of Wendell Berry that
we can be joyful though we know the facts

that *Hamlet* still resonates in the year of COVID
as we ponder our own mortality and consider
this quintessence of dust

that when cancer goes into remission
worry still lingers
like scorched kernels of popped corn

that Little Richard's *Good Golly, Miss Molly*
was not the type of music a convent nun
of the fifties wanted for her good Catholic girls

that there exist a hundred sextillion stars, from which
the Star of Bethlehem broke through in 2020
to give hope to our pandemic-weary world

that our world is hurting

that we could do more chuffing.

ODE TO SPRING

O grave, where is your victory?
O death, where is your sting?
—1 Corinthians 15:55

Open the door to springtime,
to strawberries debuting
in raised beds of earth,
their red heads peaking
from under tender foliage.
Greet show-stopping tulips,
chins up and chests out,
standing at attention, ready
to salute the sky. Throw the gate wide
to mockingbirds' early morning trills,
to tender Zephyr winds and caressing
sun and April's rain on clothes
and eyelashes. Hail the budding
birches, skint from winter's abuse,
birds' nests high on naked branches,
moss embedding trunks like inkblots.
Welcome Ruby Reds and Pink Lace
and ornamental dogwoods, their blood-
stained flowers and crown of thorns
acclaiming another spring,
another open door.

NEW YEAR'S EVE, 2020

Today I will give thanks
for the glass brimming
for the one half full
for moments of exile
(a year, for that matter)
for miracles that appear
in the night; for strangers'
prayers,
their intercessions
a sweet aroma
causing God's nostrils to tingle;
for birthdays and anniversaries;
for summer nights, the rain warm
like mothers' milk;
for winter's gully washers
and low-moaning mountain groans
and darkness that we may know
light; for solitude that breaks
into sounds of bassoons and laughter
and obstreperous celebration;
for sisters who stand with you
and by you and for you,
who will set you straight;
for a new year's possibilities;
for forgiveness and pardon and
grace, yes, for unmerited grace.
Thank you, thank you.

ACKNOWLEDGEMENTS

Thanks to the editors and journals where the following poems first appeared, sometimes in earlier versions:

"Absalom" in *The Ekphrastic Review* (Canada).

"A Father's Day Story, 1939" in *Frost Review* (USA).

A Father's Ringworm Treatment, 1947 in *Verse Virtual* (USA).

"The Best is Yet to Come" in *The Ekphrastic Review* (Canada).

"Berlin, 1945" in *Redheaded Stepchild* (USA).

"Blackberry Cooking" in *Literary North* (USA).

"Breathless" in *Poets Online* (USA).

"Camp Meetin'" in *Heart of Flesh Literary Journal* (USA).

"Elijah" in *Heart of Flesh Literary Journal* (USA).

"Epithalamium for the Seeders" in *The Ekphrastic Review* (Canada).

"Flakhelfer" in *Heart of Flesh Literary Journal* (USA).

"For Your Glory" in *Heart of Flesh Literary Journal* (USA).

"Judas" in *The Ekphrastic Review* (Canada).

"Lamentations Upon the Death of a Nation" in *Literary North* (USA).

"New Year's Eve, 2020" in *Poets Online* (USA).

"Ode to Spring" in *Silver Birch Press* (USA).

"Race to Work, 1968" in *Silver Birch Press* (USA).

"Red Bluff, 2020" in *Global Poemic* (USA).

"Revelation" in *The Ekphrastic Review* (Canada).

"Salome" in *The Ekphrastic Review* (Canada).

"Singing the Blues" in *Heart of Flesh Literary Journal* (USA).

"Strange Fire" in *The Ekphrastic World Anthology,* 2020, Lorette C. Luzajic, ed.

"Swimming Lesson" in *The Ekphrastic Review* (Canada).

"Under the Big Top" in *The Ekphrastic Review* (Canada).

Jo Taylor is a retired, 35-year English teacher from Georgia. Her favorite genre to teach high school students was poetry, and today she dedicates more time to writing it, her major themes focused on family, place, and faith. She says she writes to give testimony to the past and to her heritage. She has been published in several journals, both on-line and in print.